The Ultimate Book of **TRIVIA**

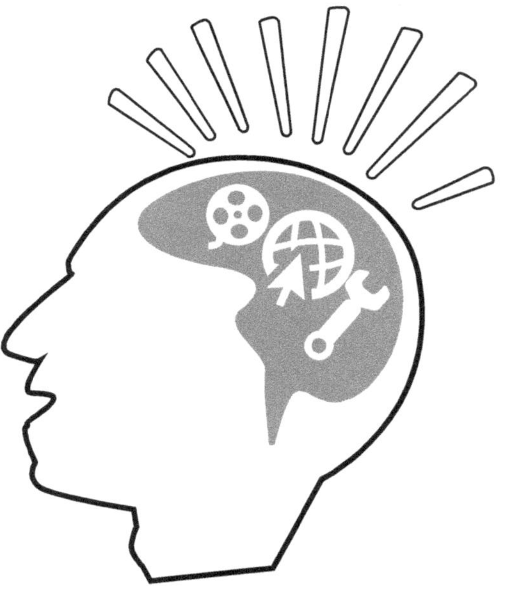

Over 1000 Exciting Trivia for a Highly Effective Brain Challenge

JAJA Books

Are you a trivia fan, or simply want an exciting brain challenge with trivia questions? This book covers almost every interesting subject: art, entertainment, science, history, sports, geography, animals and many more. All trivia questions and answers in this book have been designed with a high contrast, which makes them perfect for all ages, including the visually impaired. Answers are well arranged at the back of the book.

Published by: Brain Workouts
Printed and Bound in USA

ISBN: 9781793961808

A SPECIAL REQUEST

Thank you for your support. A simple review on amazon product page of this very special book will be helpful for us.

1. Who is the Canadian singer-songwriter best known for her hit song, "Call Me Maybe"?

2. In fluid dynamics, what is the term for the highest attainable speed an object can reach as it falls?

3. South Africa completely surrounds which other African nation?

4. Europe is separated from Asia by which mountain range?

5. In the movie "The Wizard of Oz", what did the Scarecrow want from the wizard?

6. In what year did McDonald's started serving breakfast with the introduction of the Egg McMuffin?

7. Founded in 1607, what is considered to be the first permanent English settlement in the New World?

8. Which of the traditional five senses are dolphins believed not to possess?

9. Which actress played identical twins in the 1998 movie remake of The Parent Trap?

10. What is the largest country in North America?

11.   A flamboyance is a group of what animals?

12.   What is professional wrestler John Cena's famous catchphrase?

13.   The Chihuahua is a breed of dog believed to originate from what country?

14.   The use of chopsticks originated in what country?

15.   What is a group of whales called?

16.   The oldest parliament in the world belongs to what country?

17.   Pupusas, handmade thick stuffed corn tortillas, are a traditional dish from what country?

18.   Which tennis player has won the most men's Grand Slam titles?

19.   Which Irish author wrote the avant-garde comic fiction, "Finnegan's Wake"?

20.   What famous dictator was assassinated on the Ides of March?

21.	What is the name of Atlanta's major league baseball team?

22.	What was the name of the U.S. mail service, started in 1860, that used horses and riders?

23.	What does the Statue of Liberty hold in her right hand?

24.	In which 1993 thriller does the protagonist violently lose his cool when a fast food restaurant will not let him order from the breakfast menu?

25.	Who is the only athlete ever to play in a Super Bowl and a World Series?

26.	The term "déjà vu" comes from what language?

27.	What is the colloquial term for a rotating tray often placed on a table to aid in distributing food?

28.	In hockey, how many players from each team are allowed to be on the ice at the same time?

29.	The Great Pyramid of Giza is located in what Egyptian city?

30.	According to NBA rules how long does a player have after catching the ball to shoot a free throw?

31. Which of the great lakes does not share a border with Canada?

32. The first-person shooter video game Doom was first released in what year?

33. What is the real name of the former wrestler turned actor who went by the ring name "The Rock"?

34. What is the proper term for a group of parrots?

35. Who is the lead singer for the American rock band Pearl Jam?

36. Who wrote the Pledge of Allegiance of the United States?

37. What is the name of the 1978 movie, starring Brad Davis, about an American college student who is sent to a Turkish prison for attempting to smuggle hashish out of Turkey?

38. What luxury British automobile brand was purchased by Tata motors in 2008?

39. What popular soda beverage was originally developed as a mixer for whiskey?

40. Which country won the 2012 UEFA European Championship?

41. What is the name of the actress who plays Hermione Granger in the Harry Potter series of films?

42. How many furlongs are there in one mile?

43. What was the name of the U.S. research and development project to create nuclear weapons in WWII?

44. What is the national language of India?

45. What was the name of Seattle grunge band Nirvana's first album, released in 1989?

46. In the Disney movie "Beauty and the Beast", what is the name of Gaston's bumbling sidekick?

47. The ancient Greek statue Aphrodite of Milos, better known as Venus de Milo, is currently on display in what museum?

48. What does the acronym "lol" stand for when used in phone texts and on the internet?

49. What is the largest island in the Caribbean Sea?

50. What is the unit of length that is approximately 3.26 light-years?

51.   What animal has the largest ears?

52.   Who came up with the theories of General and Special relativity?

53.   In sports, what does the acronym MVP stand for?

54.   What is the national animal of Scotland?

55.   Which is the most abundant metal in the earth's crust?

56.   What was the name of the first U.S. space station?

57.   In what year was Alfred Hitchcock's psychological thriller "Psycho" released?

58.   What is the second most abundant element in the earth's atmosphere?

59.   In the United States, where can alligators and crocodiles be found together in the wild?

60.   What are the four houses at Hogwarts School of Witchcraft and Wizardry?

61.   What was the name of the kleptomaniac monkey in the Disney movie "Aladdin"?

62.   What was the original flavor of the filling in Twinkies?

63.   What is the largest 3-digit prime number?

64.   Which psychologist investigated obedience using electric shocks?

65.   What vitamin is produced when a person is exposed to sunlight?

66.   What are the names of the three fairies in the Disney classic "Sleeping Beauty"?

67.   What is the name for a protein that acts as a biological catalyst?

68.   What is Michael J. Fox's middle name?

69.   Sauerkraut is made from what finely cut vegetable?

70.   Who is the author of the novella "The Metamorphosis", first published in 1915?

71.   Who played James Bond in the 1969 film "On Her Majesty's Secret Service"?

72.   Quasimodo is a fictional character from what novel?

73. Keiko is the name of a whale that appeared in what 1993 American family drama film?

74. The Simpsons first debuted as a short in what American variety television show?

75. Which planet in our solar system has the most oxygen?

76. Which team did the Chicago Cubs play in the 1945 World Series?

77. Shinto is the indigenous faith of what country?

78. What is the most popular breed of dog in the United States?

79. Who was the first Latin American born player to play in Major League Baseball?

80. Which city in the United States is known as the "Windy City"?

81. What is a group of lions called?

82. The Starry Night is an oil on canvas painted by which post-impressionist painter?

83. What are the five boroughs of New York City?

84. Who was the first pinch hitter to score a home run in World Series play?

85. The longest snake ever held in captivity belongs to what species?

86. In what city would you find the La Brea Tar Pits?

87. Who played the female lead role in the 1986 sci-fi movie "Aliens"?

88. What do you call a group of unicorns?

89. How many hearts does an octopus have?

90. Napoleon suffered defeat at Waterloo in what year?

91. What city is the capital of China?

92. What is the name for a confection that consists primarily of sugar or honey and almond meal?

93. In what year was the first Apple computer released?

94. What city is the capital of Canada?

95. Which bird is often associated with delivering babies?

96.   What is the sleepiest animal in the world, sleeping around 22 hours each day?

97.   In a website browser address bar what does "www" stand for?

98.   Long Island is a part of which US state?

99.   According to Guinness World Records, which author has the most published works?

100.   Each of a classic Rubik's Cube six faces is covered by how many stickers?

101.   The European Organization for Nuclear Research is known by what four letter acronym?

102.   Barack Obama was first elected president of the United States in what year?

103.   Brazil was once a colony of which European country?

104.   The final link of the first transcontinental railroad across the United States was completed in which state?

105.   What American singer-songwriter wrote and first recorded the song "Blue Suede Shoes" in 1955?

106. Who painted a late 15th-century mural known as the Last Supper?

107. What is the melting point of ice in Fahrenheit?

108. What country was host to the 1930 inaugural FIFA Football World Cup?

109. Who played the title character in the teen sitcom musical comedy "Hannah Montana"?

110. The cooking technique that involves submerging food in a liquid at a relatively low temperature is called what?

111. What is the most popular board game of all time?

112. Yerevan, one of the world's oldest continuously inhabited cities, is the capital of what country?

113. Polar bears feed mainly on what animal?

114. What sunglasses did Tom Cruise wear in the 1986 movie "Top Gun"?

115. Singer-songwriter George Michael, famous for such hits as "Faith" and "Father Figure", passed away in what year?

116. What was the first commercial product that had a Barcode?

117. Who wrote and recorded the one hit wonder "Spirit in the Sky" released in late 1969?

118. What are the names of the two actors whose characters get stuck traveling together in the movie "Trains Planes & Automobiles"?

119. Which branch of physics is devoted to the study of heat and related phenomena?

120. Hopalong Cassidy is a fictional cowboy hero, what was the name of his horse?

121. What are the seven base units of measurement in the metric system?

122. How many super bowls have the Denver Broncos won?

123. What is the name of the actress who played the Unsinkable Molly Brown in the 1997 movie Titanic?

124. What is the capital of Iceland?

125. What is a group of rhinoceros called?

126. The Alaskan Malamute is a type of what?

127.   Rod Sterling created what famous science fiction television show?

128.   The Stanley Cup is a championship trophy awarded annually to the playoff winner in what sport?

129.   What does the acronym "NASA" stand for?

130.   What is the largest lake in Africa?

131.   What did the letters of the former communist country U.S.S.R. stand for?

132.   What is the main dialect of Chinese spoken in Hong Kong by the majority of the locals?

133.   What is the name of the deepest known location in the Earth's oceans?

134.   What is the tallest building in New York?

135.   What was the full name of British novelist C. S. Lewis?

136.   What sport does Cristiano Ronaldo play?

137.   Which Patriot leader organized the Boston Tea Party in 1773?

138.   In what type of restaurant would you typically find the condiment wasabi?

139. What was the first ever series to air on the Disney Channel?

140.   In French cuisine, what is the name for the following: béchamel sauce, espagnole sauce, hollandaise sauce, tomato sauce, and velouté sauce?

141. What was the highest selling album of the 1980s in the United States?

142.   How many planets in our solar system have moons?

143. Canada's highest mountain is located in which province or territory?

144. What layer of the atmosphere lies between the troposphere and mesosphere?

145.   In what year did Fidel Castro die?

146.   How many times zones are in Canada?

147.   What does the "B" stand for in Lyndon B. Johnson?

148. In what year did Nintendo release its first game console in North America?

149.	In what year did India gain its independence from Britain?

150.	How do you say "I love you" in Italian?

151.	What is a baby turkey called?

152.	In what year was the "Perfect 10" scoring system in gymnastics abandoned?

153.	Who was the mayor of New York City during the September 11 attacks in 2001?

154.	Which planet is furthest from the sun?

155.	What musical instrument did Sherlock Holmes play?

156.	Natural pearls are found in what sea creature?

157.	"Hallelujah" is a song written by which Canadian recording artist?

158.	Which NFL Quarterback has been to the most Super Bowls?

159.	FARC is the acronym for a guerrilla movement originating in which country?

160.	The United Kingdom's withdrawal from the European Union is commonly known as what?

161. The Commonwealth of the Bahamas gained independence in 1973 from what country?

162. What was the Roman name for the goddess Hecate?

163. "All Shook Up" is a song that topped the U.S. Billboard Hot 100 on April 13, 1957. Who was the singer?

164. What do the letters of the popular fast food chain KFC stand for?

165. Which Christopher Columbus ship ran aground on his first voyage?

166. How many US states border the Pacific Ocean?

167. What planet in our solar system has the most gravity?

168. Which ocean trench is the deepest?

169. What is the capital city of Australia?

170. Cogito ergo sum, "I think, therefore I am", is a Latin phrase by which philosopher?

171. The Passenger Pigeon, now extinct, was endemic to which continent?

172.   What was the title of Kayne West's debut album release in 2004?

173.   Portugal is bordered by what other country?

174.   Who won the Nobel Prize for Literature in 2016?

175.   Who assassinated President Abraham Lincoln?

176.   Steve Jobs, Steve Wozniak, and Ronald Wayne founded what company in 1976?

177.   The Giza Plateau can be found in what country?

178.   What is the common name for stone consisting of the mineral jadeite or nephrite?

179.   What is the largest internal organ of the human body?

180.   Mr. Pibb was a soft drink created by the Coca-Cola Company to compete with what other soft drink?

181.   The Yangtze River is entirely located in which country?

182.   What is the highest score possible in 10 pin bowling?

183.   Who was the first Tudor monarch in England?

184. Which five-times Grand Slam tennis champion tested positive for a banned substance at the 2016 Australian Open?

185. Curiosity is a car-sized rover that was launched by NASA in 2011 to explore which planet?

186. The Kingdom of Joseon was founded in 1392 in what country?

187. What is the fastest fish in the Ocean?

188. The Spanish Civil War began in what year?

189. What is name of the scale used to measure the spicy heat of peppers?

190. Who came up with the three laws of motion?

191. What was the name of Taylor Swift's first album?

192. Manga are a type of comics from what country?

193. What song by Michael Jackson contains the lyrics "Annie are you OK?

194. How many U.S. presidents were only children?

195. What is the regulation height for a basketball hoop?

196.   Which animal has the most legs?

197.   How many letters are in the modern English alphabet?

198. In which city did Rosa Parks famously refuse to give up her seat on the bus?

199.   Pho is a popular noodle soup from what country?

200.   Who designed and built the Pascaline?

201. Madagascar is an island located of the southeast coast of what continent?

202.   What is the medical term for bad breath?

203. Cruella de Vil is a character who appeared in what novel by Dodie Smith?

204. What was the name of The Lone Ranger's horse that he saved from an enraged buffalo?

205. The Pascaline, invented by Blaise Pascal in the early 17th century, was a mechanical type of what device?

206. Lake Tahoe straddles the border between which two U.S. states?

207.   How do you say "hello" in Swedish?

208.   The Kangaroo Hoppet is a long-distance cross-country skiing race that is held in which county?

209.   Frankenmuth, a U.S. city nicknamed "Little Bavaria", is located in what state?

210. In what year was the Declaration of Independence created?

211.   What year was Facebook founded?

212.   What are baby beavers called?

213.   What is the fastest land snake in the world?

214.   What is the scientific name of the common potato?

215. How many elevators does the Empire State Building have?

216.   Calisto is the name of a moon orbiting what planet in our solar system?

217.   What was the name of Michael Jackson's first solo album as an adult?

207.   How do you say "hello" in Swedish?

208.   The Kangaroo Hoppet is a long-distance cross-country skiing race that is held in which county?

209.   Frankenmuth, a U.S. city nicknamed "Little Bavaria", is located in what state?

210. In what year was the Declaration of Independence created?

211.   What year was Facebook founded?

212.   What are baby beavers called?

213.   What is the fastest land snake in the world?

214.   What is the scientific name of the common potato?

215. How many elevators does the Empire State Building have?

216.   Calisto is the name of a moon orbiting what planet in our solar system?

217.   What was the name of Michael Jackson's first solo album as an adult?

218.   Nicholas II, the last Tsar of Russia was said to have been close friends with a mystical faith healer known by what name?

219.   Penicillin is used to fight what type of infections?

220.   Which two elements on the periodic table are liquids at room temperature?

221.   In what country would you find Mount Kilimanjaro?

222.   While walking through the woods in 1941, George de Mestral was inspired by the burrs that clung to his pants to create what product?

223.   Fe is the chemical symbol for what element?

224.   What is the capital city of the Philippines?

225.   Red Vines is a popular brand of what type of candy?

226.   Who was the first Roman Catholic to be Vice President of the United States of America?

227.   John Montagu, the man credited with inventing the sandwich, held what noble title?

228.   Cubic zirconia is a synthesized material often used in place of what precious stone?

229.   Who was the first First Lady to be elected to public office?

230. According to physics, what are the four fundamental forces in nature?

231. Which animal was incorrectly rumored to bury its head in the sand when frightened?

232. The filament in an incandescent light bulb is made of what element?

233. Which is the closest galaxy to the milky way?

234. What later "Star Wars" actress had an early role in the movie "Léon: The Professional"?

235. What is the capital of the Republic of Ireland?

236. Au is the symbol for what chemical element?

237. The taste that allows us to taste savory foods is called what?

238. In what year was the 4-minute mile first achieved?

239. The paperboard "Chinese takeout" box was invented in what country?

240. Who declined the 1964 Nobel Prize for literature?

241. In computer science, what does "GUI" stand for?

242. Shaquille Rashaun O'Neal retired in 2011 from what sport?

243. In what city was Ludwig van Beethoven born?

244. Abraham Lincoln was assassinated in what year?

245. Geelong is a port city located in what country?

246. Robin Williams won an Academy Award for best supporting actor in which 1997 film about a South Boston janitor?

247. In database programming, SQL is an acronym for what?

248. How do you say hello in Mandarin Chinese?

249. The Grand Slam tournaments are the four most import annual events in which two sports?

250. The State of Israel was founded in what year?

251. Schrödinger's cat is a thought experiment dealing with which type of mechanics?

252. In the late 1890s, Bayer marketed a cough, cold & pain remedy that contained what now illegal drug?

253. What is the name of Mickey Mouse´s dog?

254.   The famous Actress Winona Ryder had what last name at birth?

255. What is the smallest and most endangered species of sloth?

256. In Russia, a woman's last name usually ends in what letter?

257.   The Black Forest is located in what European country?

258.   The assassination that is said to have led to World War I, occurred in what city?

259.   Tom Hanks played "Captain Miller" in what legendary World War II movie?

260.   Who was the first NASA astronaut to visit space twice?

261. In what year did Paul McCartney announce he was quitting the Beatles?

262.   El Clásico is the name given to football (soccer) matches between which two teams?

263.   BB-8 is an astromancy droid from what film franchise?

264. What is the third most abundant gas in Earth's atmosphere?

265.   Where was the very first Hard Rock Cafe opened?

266.   What is the capital city of Croatia?

267.   Porsche is a brand of car that originated in what country?

268.   In what year was Nelson Mandela released from prison?

269. Finish this phrase: You drive for show, but putt for "______"?

270.   Ireland suffered the Great Famine beginning in 1845
due to the collapse of what crop?

271.   What type of bridge is the Golden Gate Bridge?

272.   What is the first book of the bible?

273.   Sinterklaas is the Dutch version of what mythical figure?

274.   Margarine is sold as a replacement for what?

275.   The original Ghostbusters movie was released in June of
what year?

276.   Which book was famously rejected by 12 publishers
before finally being accepted by Bloomsbury?

277.   NASCAR is an acronym for what family-owned and
operated business?

278. Which hockey player has won the most Stanley Cups with 11 wins?

279. Which city is located both in Asia and Europe?

280. Chimichurri is a green sauce that originated in what country?

281. Who is considered the father of psychoanalysis?

282. Who was the author of "The Amityville Horror" published in 1977?

283. What city is the capital of India?

284. Our solar system is located in what galaxy?

285. Who was the first US President to declare war?

286. Who directed the movie "Harry Potter and the Prisoner of Azkaban"?

287. In science, how long is an eon?

288. Who was the first person to climb Mount Everest?

289. Diamonds are made up almost entirely of what element?

290.	What is the largest organ of the human body?

291.	How many US Supreme Court justices are there?

292.	Which character in the anime Attack on Titan is referred to as "Humanity's Strongest Soldier"?

293.	What famous horse won the Triple Crown in 1973?

294.	In what city does SpongeBob SquarePants live?

295.	Tiger Woods became a professional golfer in what year?

296.	What is the chemical symbol for Helium?

297.	How do you say goodbye in Spanish?

298.	What is a group of owls called?

299.	What is the capital of Peru?

300.	How many hydrogen atoms are in one molecule of water?

301.	Orson Welles provided the voice for which Transformer in "The Transformers: The Movie" released in 1986?

302.	Which US president was known as "The Great Communicator"?

303. What is a traditional fermented Korean side dish made seasoned vegetables and salt?

304. Catalonia is a region of what country?

305. CERN launched the very first website in what year?

306. What was the name of Robert E. Lee's most famous horse?

307. Who played Dracula in the 1931 vampire-horror film "Dracula"?

308. In which US state would you find Stone Mountain Park?

309. A teetotaler is a person that never drinks what?

310. Who was the first human to travel into space?

311. A tandoor is a type of what?

312. A pug is a cross between which two dog breeds?

313. How do you say "hello" in German?

314. Malcolm Little was a civil rights activist better known by what name?

315.   How many states are needed to ratify an amendment for it to become part of the constitution?

316.   What is the name of Washington Irving's 1819 short story about a man that fell asleep in the woods for 20 years?

317.   What is the name for the Greek goddess of victory?

318.   Who was the female lead in the movie "Titanic"?

319. In what year did the Apollo 7 human spaceflight take place?

320.   What day is Thanksgiving celebrated in Canada?

321.   Sodium chloride is most commonly called what?

322.   Which mammal has the longest gestation period?

323.   Kinnikinnick is a Native American herbal mixture used as a substitute for what?

324.   The use of reflected sounds to locate objects is known as what?

325.   The Southern Ocean surrounds which continent?

326.   The Statue of Liberty was a gift to the United States from which country?

327.   Kopi luwak is a very expensive type of what?

328.   Who wrote the 1936 novel "Gone with the Wind"?

329.   The Arabian camel, also called dromedary, has how many humps?

330.   In what month is the longest day in the Northern Hemisphere?

331.   In the world of video games, what does NES stand for?

332.   Robert James "Bobby" Fischer is a famous champion of what game?

333.   What is the world's largest active volcano?

334.   What is the word for "Hello" in Spanish?

335.   Who is the current supreme leader of North Korea?

336.   Which actor that once played James Bond previously competed in the Mr. Universe bodybuilding competition?

337.   What is the fear of clowns called?

338.   Which team won the 2016 Super Bowl?

339.   Who played the fictional anti-hero Deadpool in the 2016 movie?

340.   Guinness beer was first brewed in which country?

341.   Who is the author of the book "A Brief History of Time"?

342.   In most countries it is illegal to call sparkling wine by what name unless it was produced in certain region of France?

343.   The duck billed platypus is native to what country?

344.   How many furlongs are in a mile?

345.   The Electoral College in the United States is made up of how many electors?

346.   What is the highest number of Michelin stars a restaurant can receive?

347.   Who was the first emperor of China?

348.   How many keys are on most baby grand pianos?

349.   Which actor played the main character in the 1990 film "Edward Scissorhands"?

350.   What does the acronym DNA stand for?

351. Gymnophobia is the fear of what?

352. A person able to use both hands with equal skill is called what?

353. Superman is a fictional superhero from what fictional planet?

354. Canada is made up of how many provinces?

355. Who was the lead singer of the band Audioslave?

356. What do the letters in NCAA, the name of the association that regulates athletes, stand for?

357. Snoopy from the comic peanuts is what breed of dog?

358. Which artist is credited with developing linear perspective?

359. What is the oldest city in the United States?

360. Which political party promotes individual liberty, free markets, non-interventionism and limited government?

361. Who directed the movie "Reservoir Dogs"?

362. Which state of the United States is the smallest?

363.   Who wrote the fairy tale "The Ugly Duckling"?

364.   What natural phenomena are measured by the Richter scale?

365.   What is the chemical formula for ozone?

366.   Diana Prince is the public persona of which fictional superhero?

367.   Who was the lead singer for the rock and roll band "The Crickets"?

368.   Gumbo is a stew that originated in which state?

369.   The companies HP, Microsoft and Apple were all started in a what?

370.   Now extinct, what shark is thought to have been the largest ever on Earth?

371.   In the 1986 blockbuster "Top Gun" which actress played Goose's wife?

372.   According to Greek mythology which Gorgon had snakes for hair and could turn onlookers into stone?

373.   The US military installation Area 51 is located in which state?

374.   In What state was President Barack Obama born?

375.   Who was the oldest person to sign the Declaration of Independence?

376.   New Orleans is known as the birthplace of what type of music?

377.   What French sculptor created the Statue of Liberty?

378.   The Great Gatsby was written by which author?

379.   In what year was Queen Elizabeth II born?

380.   An octopus can fit through any hole larger than its what?

381.   On the hit show Seinfeld what was Kramer's first name?

382.   Which pop star sang the national anthem at the 50th Super Bowl?

383.   Most adults have how many canine teeth?

384.   Who played Batman in the 1989 Tim Burton version of the film?

385.   The meat of a game animal, such as deer, is called what?

386.   The Walker Law passed in 1920 in New York was a law
regulating which sport?

387.   How many acres are in a square mile?

388.   What is the name of the main protagonist in the Legend
of Zelda series of video games?

389.   What is the smallest planet in our solar system?

390.   Who was the shortest player ever to play in the NBA?

391.   In what year did the French revolution begin?

392.   Which artist created the sculpture "The Thinker"?

393.   Which shark is the biggest?

394.   Fonts that contain small decorative lines at the end of a
stroke are known as what?

395.   What language do they speak in Brazil?

396.   How many feet are in a mile?

397.	What takes an average of 8 minutes 20 seconds to reach the Earth?

398.	The Artful Dodger is a character from which novel?

399.	What did the famous Hollywood sign, located in Los Angeles, originally say?

400.	Where is the lowest point, on dry land, on the earth located?

401.	Who was the lead singer of the rock band Queen?

402.	Where did the sport of curling originate?

403.	The psychological test of human emotions and personality, using inkblots, is formally known as what?

404.	What ingredient in bread causes it to rise?

405.	Saint Patrick's Day was originally associated with what color?

406.	In which U.S. state would you find Mount Rushmore?

407.	In what year was the iPhone first released?

408. Who was the last professional hockey player to play without a helmet?

409. The range of frequencies over which electromagnetic radiation extends is known as what?

410. Which two countries share the longest undefended border?

411. The Roman numeral "L" stands for what number?

412. Which Teenage Mutant Ninja Turtle always wears red bandanas?

413. A shuttlecock is used in what sport?

414. Who painted the famous Dutch Golden age painting "The Night Watch"?

415. Which animal has the longest tongue relative to its total size?

416. The United States is made up of how many states?

417. Which U.S. president signed Father's Day into law?

418. In what year was the first Harry Potter movie released?

419. What island does the Statue of Liberty stand on?

420.   What color do you get when you mix yellow and blue?

421.   What is the name of the instrument used to measure earthquakes?

422.   What city is the capital of Hungary?

423.   What was the first toy advertised on television?

424.   What is the national dish of Scotland?

425.   ABBA was a pop group from what country?

426.   What is the plural of the word crisis?

427.   What was the first music video played on MTV?

428.   By area, what is the smallest ocean in the world?

429.   Who was the first billionaire in the United States?

430.   What are the full names of the four members of the Beatles?

431.   What is the perceived decrease in air temperature felt by the body due to the flow of air known as?

432. In movies, a clue or piece of information which is intended to be misleading, is known as what?

433. What is the Spanish word for a heated tortilla filled with cheese?

434. The Lone Star State is the nickname for which U.S. State?

435. How many chambers are there in a dog's heart?

436. What is the slang military term for the distance of one kilometer?

437. How many years are in a score?

438. Who was at the top of Forbes 2015 list of the richest people in the world?

439. In the United States which breed of dog is commonly known as a firehouse dog?

440. What canal connects the Pacific Ocean to the Atlantic Ocean?

441. How many Olympic Games have been hosted in Africa?

442. When referring to computer memory, what does that acronym RAM stand for?

443.   Who was awarded the first United States patent for the telephone?

444.   In what year was the movie "Grease" released?

445.   Which liquor is made from the blue agave plant?

446.   In what country did table tennis originate?

447.   Which building, completed in 1653 at a cost of 32 million Rupees, took 22 years to build?

448.   The fear of being in a commitment or getting married is known as what?

449.   Who was the last man to walk on the moon?

450.   Which desert is the largest in the world?

451.   What is known as the "master gland" of the human body?

452.   Who gave the state of Florida its name?

453.   What is the Japanese word that means "empty orchestra"?

454.   What is the fastest bird in the world when in its hunting dive?

455.   What do the letters HTML, a markup language used to create web pages, stand for?

456.   Madeira, an archipelago located in the Atlantic Ocean, is autonomous region of which country?

457.   When adjusted for inflation, which is the highest grossing film of all time?

458.   In what year did the Titanic sink?

459.   Who was the Spanish surrealist painter best known for his work "The Persistence of Memory"?

460.   What animal is the symbol of the United States democratic party?

461.   What is a baby swan called?

462.   The theory that Earth's outer shell is divided into plates that glide over the mantle is known as what?

463.   Which basketball team did Michael Jordan play for in college?

464.   Which city has the largest population in the world?

465.   What city hosted the 2012 Summer Olympics?

466.   Which band sang the hit "Hey There Delilah", which reached No. 1 on the Billboard Hot 100 in 2007?

467.   Paella, a famous rice dish, originated in what country?

468.   With over 17 million units produced, what was the highest selling single model of personal computer ever?

469.   Which famous American musician was fatally shot by his father on April 1, 1984?

470.   Which is the most widely spoken language in the world?

471.   Who wrote the novel "Moby-Dick"?

472.   Valletta is the capital of what Mediterranean country?

473.   The art of paper folding is known as what?

474.   What was the name of the 1999 American found footage horror film about three student filmmakers that disappeared in the woods?

475.   Who is credited with inventing the first mechanical computer?

476.   The phrase "Let them eat cake" is commonly attributed to whom?

477. What four states of matter are observable in everyday life?

478. What is the chemical symbol for table salt?

479. Who is the voice of Spongebob Squarepants?

480. Which city is traditionally said to be built on seven hills?

481. In which national park would you find the geyser known as "Old Faithful"?

482. What is the hottest planet in our solar system?

483. Who is generally acknowledged as the "father" of the modern periodic table?

484. Which President is on the United States 1,000 dollar bill?

485. What animal has the fastest metabolism?

486. Which Olympic sport was featured in the movie "Cool Runnings"?

487. Which country has the most volcanoes?

488. What is the capital of Quebec Canada?

489. Where was the fortune cookie invented?

490. Who wrote an ancient Chinese military treatise known as "The Art of War"?

491. What is the name of the Spanish islands that lie off the Northwest coast of Africa?

492. A koala's diet consists mainly of what?

493. Who wrote "The Little Mermaid"?

494. Which element, previously used in the production of felt, lead to the expression "mad as a hatter"?

495. What capital city lies on the Potomac River?

496. What is it called when a star, possibly cause by a gravitational collapse, suddenly increases greatly in brightness?

497. The slogan "Just Do It" was created in 1988 for which company?

498. Who was the first actor to play Doctor Who in the television series?

499. Which is the largest of Mars' two moons?

500. Which actor played the captain of the Enterprise in the television series "Star Trek the Next Generation"?

501. The study of fossils other than anatomically modern humans is known as what?

502. In what year was the first James Bond film "Dr. No" released?

503. Jules Verne's fictional submarine the Nautilus is captained by which character?

504. Which US Holiday is celebrated on October 12th?

505. An animal that lives part of its life on land and part in water is known as what?

506. World War I flying ace Manfred von Richthofen is known by what nickname?

507. What was the first governing document of the Plymouth Colony signed aboard ship on November 11, 1620?

508. How many paintings did Vincent Van Gogh sell during his lifetime?

509. Bruce Willis played a convict turned time traveler in what 1995 movie?

510. In 1781, what was the first planet to be discovered using the telescope?

511. Which elements symbol is the letter K on the periodic table?

512. What is a baby rabbit called?

513. What is the world's largest ocean?

514. Of the four rocky planets in our solar system, which is the largest and most dense?

515. Which planet has the most moons?

516. In the US, a pint of milk is equal to how many cups of milk?

517. 1,024 Gigabytes is equal to one what?

518. Which animal has the longest gestation period?

519. What is the capital of North Korea?

520. In which US city was Walt Disney born?

521. What was the first feature film originally presented with sound?

522. What are the first three words of the bible?

523. In which country is the Nobel Peace Prize awarded?

524. In what year was the original "Jurassic Park" film released?

525. Which animal has the largest brain?

526. How many Super Bowl Rings did Troy Aikman win?

527. Who led the first expedition to sail around the world?

528. What US state has the longest official name?

529. In the movie "Back to the Future", what speed did the DeLorean need to reach in order to achieve time travel?

530. Which planet in our solar system spins the fastest?

531. Who was the first person selected as Time Magazine's Man of the Year?

532. The French Cote D'Azur is known as what in English?

533. Who is remembered for his large and stylish signature on the United States Declaration of Independence?

534. In 1998, what Major League Baseball player broke the single season home run record previously set by Roger Maris?

535. The highest temperature ever recorded in the United States occurred in which State?

536.   What does the Japanese phrase, "domo arigato" mean in English?

537.   Who is next in line to succeed the President, after the Vice President?

538.   On September 24, 1906 President Theodore Roosevelt established the first US national monument. What was it?

539.   Which country has the longest land border?

540.   Rapper Vanilla Ice had a hit song titled "Ice Ice Baby", from which other song did "Ice Ice Baby" sample from?

541.   What US city was the first to host the Olympic Games?

542.   What was the first wild card NFL team to win the Super Bowl?

543.   Edward Teach was a notorious English pirate better known by what nickname?

544.   Which team won the National Football League's first Super Bowl?

545.   What popular movie musical, directed by John Hutson, was released in 1982?

546. In 1967, what band released the hit song "Ruby Tuesday"?

547. The island of Great Britain is made up of what three somewhat autonomous regions?

548. In what year did Neil Armstrong and Buzz Aldrin land on the moon?

549. Who was the first president of the United States to live in the White House?

550. New York City was originally known by which Dutch name?

551. Where would you find St. Peter's Basilica?

552. In 1998, what Major League Baseball player broke the single season home run record previously set by Roger Maris?

553. In the movie "The Lion King", what was Simba's mother's name?

554. A young woman in the 1920s that behaved and dressed boldly was referred to as what?

555. On what continent would you not find bees?

556. In 1893, which country became the first to give women the right to vote?

557. Which actor was the voice of Darth Vader in the original Star Wars films?

558. In what year was the blue M&M first introduced?

559. How old must a person be to run for President of the United States?

560. At what temperature are Celsius and Fahrenheit equal?

561. In which Star Wars film did the Ewoks first appear?

562. In what year did the Houston Texans become a team in the US National Football League?

563. Which US city has been hit by the most tornadoes?

564. In what year was the Chevrolet Chevelle first produced?

565. The desire to eat strange things that are non-nutritive is known as what?

566. What was the first capital city of the United States?

567. How many holes are there in a full round of golf?

568. The fans of Taylor Swift are known as what?

569. Who is the author of The Hobbit and the Lord of the Rings trilogy?

570. Marie Curie was the first person to win two of what prize?

571. What does the French phrase, "répondez, s'il vous plait," known by the acronym RSVP mean in English?

572. In what year did the aviator Charles A. Lindbergh cross the Atlantic Ocean?

573. What are the names of the two Muppet characters that heckle the rest of the cast from their balcony seats?

574. How many people have walked on the moon?

575. How much money is a US Olympic gold medalist awarded?

576. Sicily is the largest island in which sea?

577. What type of animal is the mascot for the Oakland Athletics baseball team?

578. Which music group has received the most Grammy Awards?

579. What do golfers shout to warn other golfers when they hit an errant shot?

580.   What are the four main ingredients in beer?

581. Which country and its territories cover the most time zones?

582.   Bubble tea originated in which country?

583.   Which one of the seven ancient wonders of the world is still standing today?

584.   What date is Cinco de Mayo celebrated in the United States?

585. Who was the first Spaniard to set foot in what is now the US state of Florida?

586. In the movie "Bambi", what type of animal is Bambi's friend Flower?

587. What was the first department store to open in the United States?

588. Which actress played the role of Mary (adult) in the movie "It's a Wonderful Life"?

589.   The writer Eric Blair went by what pen name?

590.   In which state of the United States would you find Fort Knox?

591.   What type of animal is known as the ship of the desert?

592.   Which country is home to the world's oldest operating amusement park?

593.   What planet in our solar system has the longest day?

594.   What country has the largest land mass?

595.   How many teams are there in the American National Football League?

596.   The teddy bear was named after what famous American politician?

597.   In what month is the Earth closest to the sun?

598.   According to Mohs scale, what mineral is the hardest?

599.   Aspirin comes from the bark of what tree?

600.   In the board game Monopoly, if you pay to get out of jail, how much does it cost?

601.   Which action movie star was the voice of the Iron Giant?

602.   What country was the first to send an object to the surface of the moon?

603.   What was the NBA player Kobe Bryant named after?

604.   According to Greek mythology, who was the goddess of beauty?

605.   In what year did Cuba formally gain it's independence from Spain?

606.   In what year was the Nintendo 64 officially released?

607.   In what month does winter begin in the Southern Hemisphere?

608.   In what year did Canada become a country?

609.   What was first feature length animated film?

610.   What city connects two continents?

611.   Which US state has the nickname the Treasure State?

612.   What is the job title of the person in charge of the camera and lighting crews working on a film?

613.   Chilean sea bass originally went by what less appetizing name?

614.   Which bone is the longest bone in the human body?

615.   What is the only sea on Earth with no coastline?

616.   In what year was the United States Pledge of Allegiance written?

617.   Which musician is often called the fifth Beatle?

618.   Who sang the version of the song "Day-O" (The Banana Boat Song) released in 1956?

619.   What football teams have never made it to the Super Bowl?

620.   How many fingers do the Simpsons cartoon characters have?

621.   At what wind speed does a tropical storm become a hurricane?

622.   What phrase, often used in typing practice, includes every letter in the English alphabet?

623.   What building is found on the back of a United States 100-dollar bill?

624.   Which US city also goes by the nickname the Big Apple?

625.   Which animal is the tallest in the world?

626. Who is the only US president to serve more than two terms?

627. Rubies and sapphires are both made of what rock-forming mineral?

628. Who is credited to be the first person to circumnavigate the globe?

629. In our solar system which two planets rotate clockwise?

630. Who was the first woman pilot to fly solo across the Atlantic?

631. What year was the two-dollar bill last printed in the United States?

632. What three planets are closest to the Sun?

633. What blood type do you need to be a universal donor?

634. What school does Harry Potter attend?

635. What does Roger mean when communicating via radio?

636. What is the US Navy's equivalent to the US Army's Basic Training?

637. Abraham Lincoln, Theodore Roosevelt and Herbert Hoover all belonged to which political party?

638. One kilobyte is equal to how many bytes?

639. What hills border Scotland and England?

640. Which 1979 film included a spaceship called Nostromo?

641. What are the ingredients in a Harvey Wallbanger cocktail?

642. In the card game poker, the acronym WSOP stands for what event?

643. What character is murdered by George in the John Steinbeck novella "Of Mice and Men"?

644. In 1939, the movie The Wizard of Oz lost the Academy Award for best picture to what film?

645. Joseph Smith was the founder of what religion?

646. Su Lin was the name given to what type of animal captured in China and brought to the United States for the first time in 1936?

647. Which painter started the impressionist movement?

648.   What is name of the world's largest and most powerful particle accelerator?

649.   What is the name of the first pizzeria to open in the United States?

650.   Who is often referred to as "the father of scuba diving"?

651.   What was the nickname for the Hughes H-4 Hercules aircraft that made a single flight in 1947?

652.   What female singer had an embarrassing wardrobe malfunction during the Super Bowl XXXVIII halftime show?

653.   The largest volcano ever discovered in our solar system is located on which planet?

654.   The island of Saipan is a commonwealth of which country?

655.   What is the tallest building in the world?

656.   What is the name given to an ancient analog computer that was discovered by divers off a Greek island in 1900?

657.   What catch phrase is most commonly associated with the actor Arnold Schwarzenegger?

658.   In which sport does the bowler deliver the ball to the batsman?

659. Lemurs, a type of primate, are native to what island nation?

660.   How many stripes are on the flag of the United States?

661.   What is the official language of the Canadian province Quebec?

662.   The lowest natural temperature ever directly recorded at ground level was measured on what Continent?

663. What famous musician was shot by Mark David Chapman in the year 1980?

664.   What was the name of the passenger train service created in 1883 that connected Paris and Constantinople?

665.   Who directed the 1977 movie Star Wars?

666.   Who invented the cotton gin in 1793, allowing for much greater cotton production?

667.   Which athlete has won the most Olympic medals?

668.   The dingo is a free ranging dog found mainly in which country?

669.   The martial art of Kung Fu originated in which country?

670.   The Communist Manifesto was written by which two German philosophers?

671.   In hockey, what is known as a hat trick?

672.   Who was the male lead in the 1996 summer blockbuster Independence Day?

673.   What painter is famous for cutting off part of his ear?

674.   Who wrote the novel "To Kill a Mockingbird", published in 1960?

675.   What is the chemical symbol for iron?

676.   Which singer rose to fame with his adaptation of the song "La Bamba" in 1958?

677.   Who painted the Sistine Chapel?

678.   What is the name of the world's highest uninterrupted waterfall and in what country is it located?

679.   What is a flock of crows called?

680. What was the name of the first manmade satellite that was launched into space in 1957?

681. What is the largest planet in our solar system?

682. Which Spanish Island is known as "The Island of Eternal Spring"?

683. What is the white part of the inside of an egg called?

684. How many moons does the planet Venus have?

685. What year was the first Super Bowl played?

686. What movie did Elvis Presley first appear in?

687. Sri Lanka is surrounded by which ocean?

688. What Harvard dropout co-founded Microsoft?

689. What are the names of the 7 dwarfs from the Disney movie "Snow White and the Seven Dwarfs"?

690. What is the closest star to the planet Earth?

691. What is the first commandment of the ten commandments?

692.   Which country lies on the border between Spain and France?

693.   In what year was the US Constitution written?

694.   What is the most abundant element in the earth's atmosphere?

695.   Where is the baseball hall of fame located?

696.   Which 1980's television hit was renamed El Coche Fantastico for its Spanish viewers?

697.   What popular beverage once contained cocaine?

698.   In what year did World War II end?

699.   What famous actor became Governor of California in 2003?

700.   What former planet was demoted to a dwarf planet in 2006?

701.   What 3 countries do not use the metric system?

702.   What was Marilyn Monroe's name at birth?

703.   How many signs are in the zodiac?

704. The second atomic bomb ever used in war-time was dropped on what city?

705. Who was the first queen of England?

706. What is the first element on the periodic table?

707. How many items are in a baker's dozen?

708. In what country would you find the Yellow River?

709. What is the Spanish word for money?

710. What 2013 science fiction blockbuster starred Sandra Bullock and George Clooney?

711. How many letters are in the Greek alphabet?

712. In what year is Columbus credited with discovering the new world?

713. How many ounces are in a US gallon?

714. What is the main ingredient in guacamole?

715. In what year was the first modern Olympic Games held?

716. What is the official currency of the country Ecuador?

717.	What famous female singer died of alcohol poisoning in 2011 at the age of 27?

718.	What is a meteor called when it reaches earth's surface?

719.	What was the name of the first electronic general-purpose computer?

720.	How many soccer players should be on the field at the same time?

721.	What is the name of the popular Australian food spread used on sandwiches, toast and pastries?

722.	What star of the movie Basketball Diaries did not win his first Oscar until 2016?

723.	What was the name of the teacher who died in the tragic Space Shuttle Challenger disaster?

724.	What city is the capital of the country Turkey?

725.	What digital currency is Satoshi Nakamoto credited with inventing?

726.	What does HTTP stand for in a website address?

727.	Who was the second president of the United States?

728.   Who was the first black baseball player to play in the major leagues?

729.   What is the chemical equation for hydrogen peroxide?

730. The United States state of Georgia is famous for what fruit?

731.   Which famous singer appeared in the movie Mad Max: Beyond Thunder dome?

732.   In which state was the first oil well drilled in the United States?

733.   What is the second largest country by land mass?

734.   What is the largest animal currently on Earth?

735.   In what ocean did the Titanic sink?

736.   Who was the first man to set foot on the moon?

737.   What planet is closest to the sun?

738.   What is the world's smallest country?

739.   What song from the Disney film "Coco" won the 2018 Academy Award for Best Original Song?

740. In the X-Men film franchise, Halle Berry played the role of which character?

741. A blunderbuss is an obsolete type of what?

742. Moss, garter, and seed are common terms used in which type of handicraft?

743. In Olympic archery, what is the standard distance of the target from the archer?

744. What is the highest number found on a standard roulette wheel?

745. Who created the comedy science fiction series, "The Hitchhiker's Guide to the Galaxy"?

746. Who was the first man to appear on the cover of Playboy Magazine?

747. Which water sport is the official state individual sport of Hawaii?

748. Spanish silver dollars, originally called the Spanish peso, were each worth how many Spanish reales?

749. What is the mathematical formula for Newton's Second Law of Motion?

750.   Which fast food restaurant chain once tested bubble gum broccoli as a children's menu item?

751.   Who directed the romantic comedy fantasy adventure film The Princess Bride?

752.   Who was first U.S. president to be impeached?

753.   What figure of speech meaning, "including everything", comes from three major parts of a musket?

754.   Ron McKernan of the Grateful Dead was commonly known by what nickname?

755.   What is the highest mountain when measured from the center of Earth?

756.   In what country were the Winter Olympics first held?

757.   Who starred alongside Eddie Albert in the television sitcom "Green Acres"?

758.   Alexander the great was taught by which Greek philosopher?

759.   In Frank Baum's novel The Wonderful Wizard of Oz, on which the film is based, what color are Dorothy's slippers?

760.   The leaning tower of Pisa is located in which city?

761. How many gifts would you receive if you received all of the gifts in the song, "The Twelve Days of Christmas"?

762.   Which is the only Disney Princess that has a child?

763.   Which bird has eyes that are larger than its brain?

764.   What are the first four digits of Pi?

765. What are the two South American countries that belong to OPEC?

766. Made up predominantly of young men, adult fans of the animated television series My Little Pony are known as what?

767.   What igneous rock has a density less than water?

768. Which city served as the capital of the United States from 1785 until 1790?

769. Published in 1906, White Fang is a novel about a wolf-dog written by which American author?

770.   What does the online acronym SMH stand for?

771. A league is equivalent to how many nautical miles at sea?

772.   What is the only snake in the world that builds a nest for its eggs?

773.   How the Grinch Stole Christmas is a 2000 American Christmas fantasy comedy film starring which actor as the Grinch?

774.   The name of the popular online battle royale game PUBG, is short for what?

775.   What is the official winter and summer sports of Canada?

776.   What is the largest country located entirely in Europe?

777.   What famous Christmas legend did a Montgomery Ward advertising man create as part of his job?

778.   Jim Davis was the cartoonist behind which widely syndicated comic strip?

779.   Who appeared on the cover of the first issue of People Magazine on March 4, 1974?

780.   American Gothic, a 1930 portrait depicting a farmer and his daughter posing in front of their house, was painted by which artist?

781.   What inland U.S. state has the longest shoreline?

782.   Who sang the title song "Grease" in the 1978 musical
motion picture?

783.   In 1863, which U.S. President declared that the last
Thursday in November should be celebrated as
Thanksgiving?

784. What heavy metal element was once known as quicksilver?

785. Which famous toy manufacturer is also the world's largest
tire manufacturer by units produced?

786. Where did a robot named Spirit remain operational over
2000 sols past its planned 90-sol mission?

787. Who ties Cloris Leachman for the most Emmys won by
a female performer?

788. A word that is spelled the same forwards and backwards
is called a what?

789.   What gives red blood cells their color?

790. Tapestry, Inc., with a stock ticker symbol of TPR is more
commonly known as what retail store and line of products?

791. Who became both a vice president and president of the
United States without ever being elected to either office?

792. When referring to an establishment that sells alcoholic drinks, what is the word "pub" short for?

793. Wrangell-St. Elias, the largest national park in the U.S., is located in which state?

794. The adult human skeleton is made of up how many bones?

795. Papua New Guinea is bordered by which country to the west?

796. What are the first names of the lip-syncing musical duo known as Milli Vanilli that earned a Grammy Award in 1990?

797. "If I Had $1000000" is a song by which Canadian musical group?

798. When referring to cables used to transmit audio/video, what does HDMI stand for?

799. What three colors appear on the flag of Ireland?

800. In 2003, which U.S. state was officially declared the birthplace of aviation?

801. The Scarlet Letter is a historical fiction novel written by which American author?

802. What "King" of golf lent his name to a mixture of iced tea and lemonade?

803. Which actor played Freddie Mercury in the 2018 film Bohemian Rhapsody?

804. What two sisters faced each other in the finals of the French Open, Wimbledon, and US Open in 2002?

805. In which Asian country is the city of Chiang Mai located?

806. A poke bowl is a diced raw fish dish that originated in which U.S. state?

807. Whose dress was dried like jerky for the Rock & Roll Hall of Fame?

808. What is the name of the Las Vegas professional ice hockey team that began play in the 2017–18 NHL season?

809. In which Disney film do two cats sing "The Siamese Cat Song"?

810. What late "Enter the Dragon" star would have been age 32 at the film's Hong Kong premiere?

811. Notorious Colombian drug lord Pablo Escobar died in a shootout in what city?

812.   What is the only mammal born with horns?

813.   Who was the first female Prime Minister of a European country?

814.   Who is the only basketball player to score 100 points in a single NBA game?

815.   Nellie Bly wrote, "What, excepting torture, would produce insanity quicker than this treatment?" in her 1887 undercover exposé of what type of institution?

816.   In what city would you find the Wizard of Oz?

817.   What is the name for the pigment found in your skin and hair that gives them color?

818.   What happened to British street artist Banksy's "Girl with Balloon" when it sold for $1.4 million at Sotheby's auction house in 2018?

819. A standard 7-inch vinyl single is usually played at what rpm?

820.   Hamburgers get their name from what European city?

821.   Who was the captain of the Mayflower when it took the Pilgrims to New England in 1620?

822.   Who holds the record for the most home runs in a single major league baseball season?

823.   Which video game studio created the popular online game Fortnite?

824.   What popular Disney movie is set near Salem, Massachusetts in the years 1693 and 1993?

825.   Who patented the concept of a flat engine or "boxer" engine in 1896?

826.   Who was the king of Britain during the American revolutionary war?

827.   In what city does a Creole lady of the night strut her stuff, according to the original 1974 song "Lady Marmalade"?

828.   The expression "oy vey" comes from what language?

829.   Where does Spongebob Squarepants work?

830.   Which U.S. president issued the Emancipation Proclamation?

831.   "Arco iris" is the Spanish term for what natural phenomenon?

832. Eddie Murphy's first major motion picture role was in what movie released in 1982 co-starring Nick Nolte?

833. What comic strip's final panel depicts a boy and a tiger sledding away?

834. What flightless bird is featured on New Zealand's one dollar coin?

835. What city is most commonly referred to as "The City of Light"?

836. The United States Supreme Court consists of how many judges?

837. What is the color of Underdog's cape?

838. Olympia is the capital city of which U.S. state?

839. What is the name of Donald Duck's sister?

840. Marxist revolutionary Che Guevara was born in what country?

841. What is Shawshank, in the movie The Shawshank Redemption?

842. What was the first publicly traded U.S. company to reach a $1 trillion market cap?

843. What was the nickname for the four engine B-17 bomber planes used during WWII?

844. Which event did US President Franklin D. Roosevelt call, "A day that will live in infamy"?

845. Naan is the Persian word for what?

846. Who is the lead singer for the rock band Guns N' Roses?

847. Which country financed Christopher Columbus' 1492 exploration?

848. Which two South American countries do not touch the sea?

849. Which U.S. state has the motto "Live Free or Die" on their license plate?

850. Foie gras is a french delicacy made from the liver of what animal?

851. What 1985-1992 sitcom earned Emmy awards for its four stars, all women over the age of 50?

852. A Boeing 777 is equipped with how many engines?

853.   What was the name of cowboy star Roy Rogers' palomino horse?

854.   In which national park would you find the geyser known as "Old Faithful"?

855.   What U.S. agency's motto is "Fidelity, Bravery, Integrity"?

856.   How many teams are in the American National Football league?

857.   What actor played Russian roulette in "The Deer Hunter", demanded "More Cowbell" on "Saturday Night Live", and danced solo in Fatboy Slim's "Weapon of Choice" video?

858.   The live action superhero television series "Mighty Morphin Power Rangers" premiered in what year?

859.   "Believe in something, even if it means sacrificing everything" is a Nike advertisement associated with what former NFL player?

860.   How many members were in the American rock band The White Stripes?

861.   Who wrote the American realist novel "The Grapes of Wrath"?

862.   What group of lakes located in upstate New York are named after a part of the human anatomy?

863.   What holiday, celebrated December 26 to January 1, is named after the Swahili word for "first"?

864.   Bogota is the high-altitude capital of which country?

865.   What Marvel character's real name is Carol Danvers?

866.   Who plays Jack Ryan in the 2002 American spy thriller "The Sum of all Fears"?

867.   What television host quipped at his 1990 wedding, "The answer is… yes"?

868.   The Trout Memo was an espionage guidebook written by what British author during WWII?

869.   In the game of pool, what is the standard color for the one ball?

870.   What future U.S. president was stranded on a desert island as a 26-year-old navy lieutenant in 1943?

871.   What was the first all-professional baseball team with salaried players?

872. In the U.S. military, what does the acronym NCO stand for?

873. The Hound of the Baskervilles is a crime novel featuring which fictional detective?

874. What six-letter magic word in comic books invokes Solomon, Hercules, Atlas, Zeus, Achilles, and Mercury?

875. Which continent is also a country?

876. Able to be seen from outer space, what is Earth's largest living structure?

877. Daniel Peggotty is a character from which Charles Dickens novel published in 1850?

878. What is the name of the sequel to the movie Wreck-It Ralph that was released in 2018?

879. What is called when a player scores two goals in a game of soccer?

880. A fortnight is a unit of time equal to how many days?

881. Originating in Germany, the Danube River empties into what body of water?

882.   Which actor played the fictional character Dr. Emmett Brown in the Back to the Future trilogy?

883.   A wombat is a marsupial native to which country?

884.   What was the name of the coffee shop in the hit sitcom friends?

885.   When referring to the test taken for entrance into the US military what does ASVAB stand for?

886.   Filipino First Lady Imelda Marcos, was famous for her very large collection of what?

887.   Who was the commander of the Confederate Army during the battle of Gettysburg?

888.   What Catholic prayer lends its name to a very long forward pass thrown with time running out in American football?

889.   On the popular social website Reddit, what does AMA stand for?

890.   A "sounder" is the term used to refer to a group of what type of animal?

891.   In what two-act ballet does a toymaker's goddaughter travel to the Land of Sweets on Christmas Eve?

892.   What do the letters CPU stand for when referring to the "brains" of a computer?

893.   Sydney Carton is the central character in what Charles Dickens novel?

894.   The Roman Catholic Church La Sagrada Familia, located in Barcelona Spain, was designed by which Catalan architect?

895.   What murder-mystery board game replaced the suspect Mrs. White with Dr. Orchid in 2016?

896.   MMA is the acronym for what full-contact combat sport?

897. Officially opened in 1869, what artificial waterway connects the Mediterranean Sea to the Red Sea?

898.   What is the capital city of South Korea?

899.   In what Mark Twain novel does an engineer from Connecticut travel back in time to the age of Camelot?

900.   On which popular website do users send tweets?

901.   Who played the fictional character Phoebe Buffay on the American sitcom Friends?

902.   Established in the 1920s, what historic double-digit highway connected Chicago and Los Angeles?

903. Which continent has the highest human population density?

904.   What automobile manufacturer was first to implement the assembly line for the mass production of an entire automobile?

905.   What is the Latin plural form of the word cactus?

906.   The aardvark is native to which continent?

907. The southernmost part of the US is located in which state?

908.   Who was the last queen of France prior to the French revolution?

909. Come as You Are, a song by the grunge band Nirvana was released on which album?

910.   According to ancient Roman religion, who was the god of the sea?

911.   Which US state has the highest number of colleges and universities?

912.   The Punisher is a fictional character appearing in comic books published by which company?

913. What common expression is used to refer to the horseshoe shaped zone found along the Pacific rim where approximately 90% of the world's earthquakes occur?

914. What is the name for the upper arm bone found in humans?

915. According to legend, Romulus and Remus founded what city?

916. The song "Eye of the Tiger" by the band Survivor was the theme song for what movie released in 1982?

917. Professional footballer Lionel Messi was born in which country?

918. What was the name of the first manned mission to land on the moon?

919. The silkscreen paintings Campbell's Soup Cans and Marilyn Diptych were created in 1962 by which American artist?

920. Saskatchewan is a province of which country?

921. The famous American writer Samuel Langhorne Clemens is better known by what pen name?

922. What is the only mammal that can truly fly?

923.   When referring to a type of music, what does R&B stand for?

924.   Ice hockey pucks are made from what material?

925.   The Carolina Reaper, Dorset Naga, and Trinidad Scorpion are varieties of what kind of edible plant?

926.   The headquarters of the United Nations is located in what city?

927.   A misandrist is a person that hates what?

928.   In the game of chess, how many pawns does each player start with?

929.   SNES is the acronym for what popular gaming console released in the early 1990s?

930.   In 2012, Magic Johnson became part owner of which Major League Baseball team?

931.   Who did Jerry Lewis partner with to form a famous comedy duo that lasted 10 years?

932.   Tenochtitlan, founded in 1324, is now known as what city?

933.   In cooking, margarine is used as a substitute for what ingredient?

934.   Located in southern Siberia, what lake is the deepest and largest freshwater lake in the world?

935.   Who was the star of the popular 80s crime drama Magnum P.I.?

936.   The tallest statue in the world as of 2018, the Spring Temple Buddha, is located in what country?

937.   Which actress played the character Annie Reed in the 1993 American romantic comedy Sleepless in Seattle?

938.   At its peak in 2004, which company had over 9000 video rental stores worldwide?

939.   What is the English translation for the name of the German automaker Volkswagen?

940.   What country is named for its location on the equator?

941.   The Bill of Rights contains how many of the first amendments to the United States Constitution?

942.   With twelve Oscar nominations and three wins, who is the most nominated male actor in Academy Awards history?

943.   What is the Spanish word for meat?

944.   What is the tallest mountain in South America?

945.   What is the secret identity of the fictional superhero Batman?

946. The Concorde was a supersonic passenger airliner flown by which two airlines?

947.   What is the world's largest coral reef system?

948.   What do the letters C and H stand for in C & H Sugar?

949. Atlantis, Paradise Island is a famous resort located on which country's coral based archipelago?

950.   Who is the only former heavyweight boxing champ to be buried in Arlington National Cemetery?

951.   In what country would you find large ancient geoglyphs known as the the Nasca Lines?

952.   What skipper lost the 1983 America's Cup and then won the Cup back in 1987?

953.   What is the name for a mammal this is born incompletely developed and usually carried in the mother's pouch?

954.   Which park is the most filmed location in the world?

955.   In boxing, what is the term for an illegal punch to the back of the head or base of the skull?

956.   The profile of General George Washington appears on what United States military decoration?

957.   In the classic board game Monopoly, how much does it cost to buy a railroad?

958.   First published in 1719, "Robinson Crusoe" is a novel written by which English writer?

959.   The world's fastest growing plant is a species of what?

960.   "Hey Boo Boo, let's go get us a pic-a-nic basket!", is a famous line often said by which cartoon character?

961.   What does the muppet Oscar the Grouch live in?

962.   What is the common term for a list of things a person would like to do before they die?

963.   Stratus, Cirrus and Cumulus are types of what?

964.   When a drink is served "on the rocks", it is served with what?

965. Who was the first woman to be inducted into the Rock and Roll Hall of Fame?

966. The 1927 New York Yankees batting order, including Babe Ruth and Lou Gehrig, was known by what nickname?

967. Jamón ibérico is a type of cured ham that is traditionally produced by which two neighboring countries?

968. Dendrophobia is the fear of what?

969. Head and Shoulders is a brand of shampoo that claims to deal with what common chronic scalp condition?

970. Quito is the capital city of which South American country?

971. Which 1993 American science-fiction adventure film had a plot that involved creating a theme park from cloned dinosaurs?

972. What is the name for meteoroids that survive entry through the atmosphere and reach Earth's surface?

973. In what sport does a jammer score a point for each opponent she skates past?

974. What is the name for the offspring of a male lion and a female tiger?

975. Who won more Academy Awards in his lifetime than any other person?

976. On the Apollo 11 moon mission, which astronaut stayed aloft in the command module while Neil Armstrong and Buzz Aldrin walked on the moon?

977. What is the longest river in Australia?

978. Mario Kart is a video game series publish by which company?

979. If a liquor is 100 proof how much alcohol does it contain by percentage?

980. In the poker game Texas Hold'em, how many cards are dealt to each player?

981. Ozeki and yokozuna are the top ranks in which sport?

982. What international event for athletes with disabilities is held in the same years and cities as the Olympic Games?

983. What was the name of Jack Nicholson's character in the 1975 American comedy-drama film "One Flew Over the Cuckoo's Nest"?

984. What Greek mathematician is considered the founder and father of Geometry?

985. What notable brand of alcohol takes its name from the romanticized, storied life of a Welsh buccaneer who routed the Spanish in an attack on Panama City in 1671?

986. Which wedding anniversary is traditionally referred to as the golden wedding anniversary?

987. What ingredient is added to white sugar to make brown sugar?

988. What is the name of the dog from the 1960s television cartoon The Jetsons?

989. What is the heaviest naturally occurring element found on Earth?

990. "My bologna has a first name" are the first words of a classic Jingle advertising what company?

991. What three countries share a border with North Korea?

992. Who was the first U.S. president that was born a citizen of the United States?

993. Which book holds the record of being the most stolen book from public libraries?

994. Which former teen idol gained popularity playing the role of Miley Stewart on the Disney Channel television series Hannah Montana?

995. In 1796 Edward Jenner developed the vaccination for what disease?

996. Florence Nightingale aided the sick and wounded during which war?

997. Cinco de Mayo celebrates the Mexican army's 1862 victory over France in what battle?

998. What spiny venous fish, common in home aquariums, has become an invasive species in the Caribbean Sea and U.S. Atlantic coastal waters?

999. Which scientist is considered the father of modern genetics?

1000. The port city of Luanda is the capital city of which African country?

1001. What is the brand name for the product that has a mascot of a muscular man with a shaved head and an earring?

1002. What is the name for the branch of mathematics dealing with lengths and angles of triangles.

1003. "A Diamond is Forever" is a famous advertising slogan created in 1947 for what company?

1004. The dingo is a type of feral dog native to which country?

1005. In the fact-based movie "21" released in 2008, students from MIT made millions by counting cards playing which card game?

1006. What is the common translation for the popular Latin phrase "carpe diem"?

1007. "What you talkin' 'bout, willis?" was a catchphrase spoken by the actor Gary Coleman on what American television show?

1008. Jack the Ripper is the name given to an unidentified serial killer that terrorized what city in 1888?

1009. "Game, set, match" is an expression used to indicate a competitor has won the game in which sport?

1010. The Canadian flag features a leaf from which type of tree?

1011.   Trevi fountain is located in the capital city of which European country?

1012.   America's Next Top Model is an American reality television show created by which former model?

1013.   According to the bible, who was the longest-lived person on Earth?

1014.   Who was the tallest actor ever to win an academy award?

1015.   Which actor played a FedEX employee that became marooned on an island in the 2000 drama film Cast Away?

1016.   In what year did the great fire of London take place?

1017.   What is the only U.S. state without a rectangular flag?

1018.   Who was the first performer at the 1969 Woodstock festival?

1019.   What is the most visited museum in Europe?

1020.   What NBA player was known as "The Pearl"?

1021.   A Moscow Mule is a type of cocktail popularly served in what?

1022.   A Shakespearean sonnet consists of how many lines?

1023.   Houses of the Holy is the fifth studio album by which English rock band?

1024.   What is the largest rodent found in North America?

1025.   Founded in 1921, this company was credited with being the first "fast food" chain?

1026.   What is the closest star to our own sun?

1027.   What was Walt Disney's middle name?

1028.   How do you say panda in Spanish?

1029.   Sukiyaki is a popular hot pot dish from what country?

1030.   Who was president of the United States when bombs were dropped on Hiroshima and Nagasaki?

1031.   Which U.S. President made the first telephone call to the moon?

1032.   What is the first "themed land" just inside the main entrance of Disneyland?

1033.   "The road to greatness can take you to the edge", is the tagline of which 2014 American drama film?

1034.   Who was the United States' leading fighter pilot of WWI with 26 victories?

1035.   How many red stripes are there on the United States flag?

1036.   What NHL hockey player was nicknamed "The Golden Jet"?

1037.   Betelgeuse and Rigel are the two giant stars in which constellation?

1038.   Which American author wrote the non-fiction novel "In Cold Blood"?

1039.   Montevideo is the capital city of which South American country?

1040.   "Michael Keaton played which Spiderman villain in the 2017 superhero movie "Spiderman: Homecoming"?"

1041.   What is the name for the longest side of a right t riangle?

1041. What is the name for the longest side of a right triangle?

1042. Which Christian missionary is said to have banished all the snakes from Ireland?

1043. Lox, often served on a bagel, is a fillet of brined what?

1044. What dog breed native to Japan has a name that translates to "little brushwood dog"?

1045. Mark Zuckerberg was one of the founders of which social networking site?

1046. "Call me Ishmael" is the opening line from what novel?

1047. What is the most common blood type in humans?

1048. What is the national sport of Japan?

1049. The Gettysburg address was a speech given by which U.S. president?

1050. What does the acronym for the German multinational company BMW stand for?

1051. What is the only bird known to fly backwards?

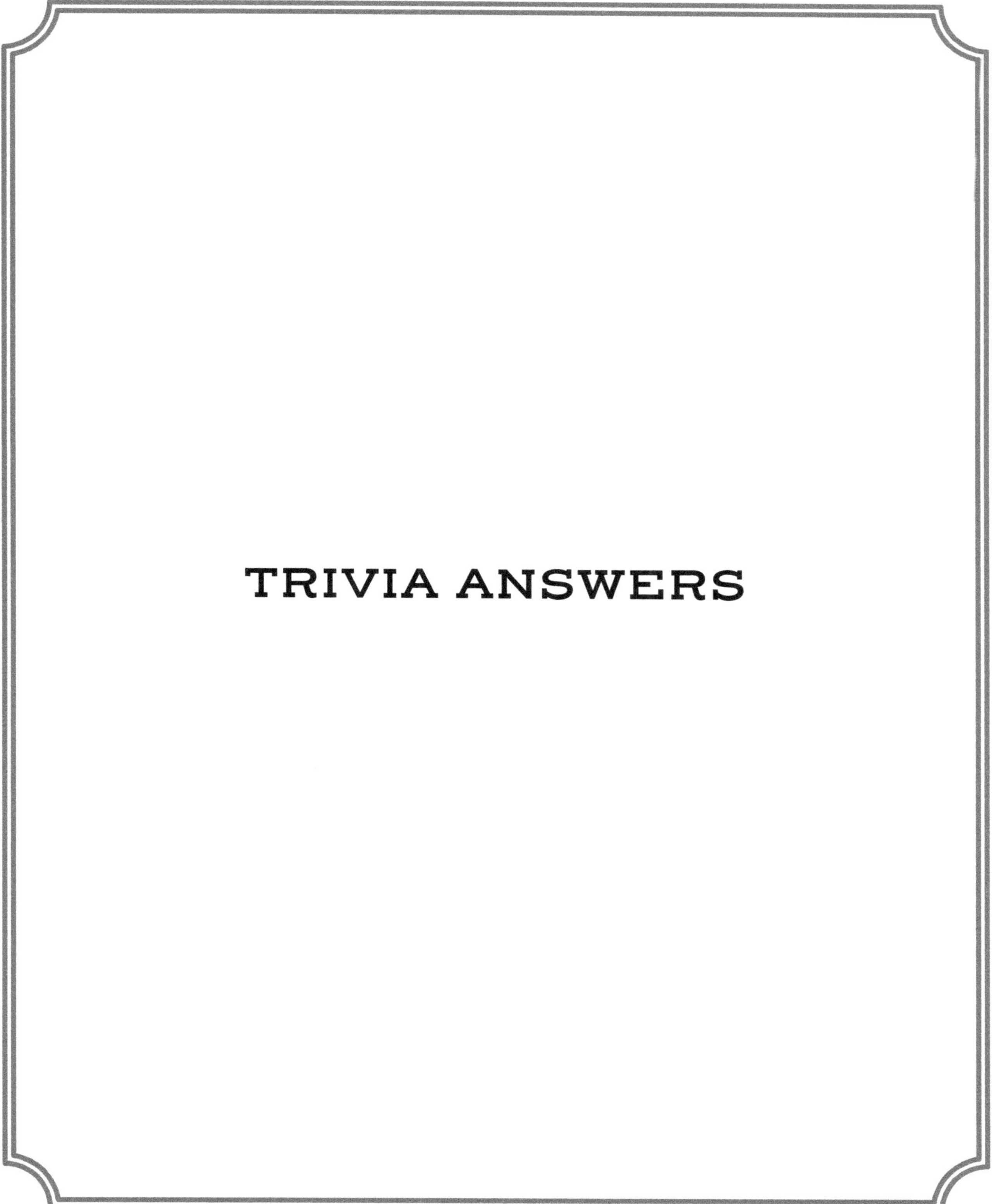

TRIVIA ANSWERS

1) Carly Rae Jepsen	29) Giza
2) Terminal Velocity	30) 10 seconds
3) Lesotho	31) Lake Michigan
4) Ural Mountains	32) 1993
5) A brain	33) Dwayne Douglas Johnson
6) 1972	34) Pandemonium
7) Jamestown, Virginia	35) Eddie Vedder
8) Smell	36) Francis Bellamy
9) Lindsay Lohan	37) Midnight Express
10) Canada	38) Jaguar
11) Flamingos	39) Mountain Dew
12) You can't see me!	40) Spain
13) Mexico	41) Emma Watson
14) China	42) Eight
15) A pod	43) Manhattan Project
16) Iceland	44) Hindi
17) El Salvador	45) Bleach
18) Roger Federer	46) LeFou
19) James Joyce	47) The Louvre in Paris, France
20) Julius Caesar	48) Laugh out loud
21) Atlanta Braves	49) Cuba
22) Pony Express	50) Parsec
23) A torch	51) Elephant
24) Falling Down	52) Albert Einstein
25) Deion Sanders	53) Most valuable player
26) French	54) Unicorn
27) Lazy Susan	55) Aluminum
28) Six	56) Skylab

57) 1960
58) Oxygen
59) South Florida
60) Gryffindor, Ravenclaw, Hufflepuff, & Slytherin
61) Abu
62) Banana cream
63) 997
64) Stanley Milgram
65) Vitamin D
66) Flora, Fauna and Merry-weather
67) Enzyme
68) Andrew
69) Cabbage
70) Franz Kafka
71) George Robert Lazenby
72) The Hunchback of Notre-Dam
73) Free Willy
74) The Tracey Ullman Show
75) Earth
76) Detroit Tigers
77) Japan
78) Labrador Retriever
79) Luis Manuel Castro
80) Chicago
81) A pride
82) Vincent van Gogh
83) Manhattan, the Bronx, Queens, Brooklyn, and Staten Island
84) Yogi Berra
85) Reticulated python
86) Los Angeles
87) Sigourney Weaver
88) A blessing.
89) Three
90) 1815
91) Beijing
92) Marzipan
93) 1976
94) Ottawa
95) Stork
96) Koala
97) World Wide Web
98) New York
99) L. Ron Hubbard
100) Nine
101) CERN
102) 2008
103) Portugal
104) Utah
105) Carl Perkins
106) Leonardo da Vinci
107) 32°F

108) Uruguay

109) Miley Cyrus

110) Poaching

111) Chess

112) Armenia

113) Seals

114) Ray Ban Aviator (RB 3025)

115) 2016

116) Wrigley's Juicy Fruit Gum

117) Norman Greenbaum

118) Steve Martin & John Candy

119) Thermodynamics

120) Topper

121) The ampere, the candela, the kelvin, the kilogram, the meter, the mole and the second

122) Three

123) Kathy Bates

124) Reykjavik

125) A "crash"

126) Dog

127) The Twilight Zone

128) Hockey

129) National Aeronautics and Space Administration

130) Lake Victoria

131) Union of Soviet Socialist

132) Cantonese

133) Challenger Deep

134) One World Trade Center

135) Clive Staples Lewis

136) Soccer (football)

137) Samuel Adams

138) Japanese

139) Good Morning, Mickey

140) Mother sauces

141) Thriller by Michael Jackson

142) Six

143) Yukon

144) Stratosphere

145) 2016

146) Six

147) Baines

148) 1985

149) 1947

150) Ti amo

151) Poult or chick

152) 2006

153) Rudy Giuliani

154) Neptune

155) Violin

156) Oyster

157) Leonard Cohen

158) Tom Brady

159) Colombia

160) Brexit

161) United Kingdom

162) Trivia

163) Elvis Presley

164) Kentucky Fried Chicken

165) La Santa Maria

166) Five states: California, Oregon, Washington, Alaska and Hawaii

167) Jupiter

168) Mariana Trench or Marianas Trench

169) Canberra

170) René Descartes

171) North America

172) The College Dropout

173) Spain

174) Bob Dylan

175) John Wilkes Booth

176) Apple Computer, Inc.

177) Egypt

178) Jade

179) Liver

180) Dr Pepper

181) The People's Republic of China

182) 300

183) Henry VII

184) Maria Sharapova

185) Mars

186) Korea

187) Sailfish

188) 1936

189) Scoville scale

190) Sir Isaac Newton

191) Taylor Swift

192) Japan

193) Smooth Criminal

194) None

195) 10 feet (3.048 m)

196) Millipede

197) 26

198) Montgomery Alabama

199) Vietnam

200) Blaise Pascal

201) Africa

202) Halitosis

203) The Hundred and One Dalmatians

204) Silver

205) Calculator

206) California & Nevada

207) Hej

208) Australia

209) Michigan

210) 1776

211) 2004
212) Kittens or Kits
213) Black Mamba
214) Solanum tuberosum L.
215) 73
216) Jupiter
217) Off The Wall
218) Grigori Rasputin
219) Bacterial
220) Mercury and Bromine
221) Tanzania
222) Velcro
223) Iron
224) Manila
225) Red licorice
226) Joe Biden
227) Earl of Sandwich
228) Diamond
229) Hillary Rodham Clinton
230) Strong Force, Electromagnetic Force, Weak Force, Gravitational Force
231) Ostrich
232) Tungsten
233) Andromeda galaxy, about 2.5 million light years away
234) Natalie Portman
235) Dublin
236) Gold
237) Umami
238) 1954 by Roger Bannister in 3:59.4
239) The United States
240) Jean-Paul Sartre
241) Graphical user interface
242) Basketball
243) Bonn, Electorate of Cologne
244) 1865
245) Australia
246) Good Will Hunting
247) Structured Query Language
248) Ni Hao
249) Tennis & Golf
250) 1948
251) Quantum Mechanics
252) Heroin
253) Pluto
254) Horowitz
255) The pygmy three-toed sloth (Bradypus pygmaeus)
256) A
257) Germany
258) Sarajevo
259) Saving Private Ryan

260) Gus Grissom
261) 1970
262) Real Madrid and FC Barcelona
263) Star Wars
264) Argon
265) Piccadilly, London
266) Zagreb
267) Germany
268) 1990
269) Dough
270) Potato
271) Suspension
272) Genesis
273) Santa Claus (Saint Nicholas)
274) Butter
275) 1984
276) Harry Potter and The Philosopher's Stone
277) The National Association for Stock Car Auto Racing
278) Henri Richard
279) Istanbul
280) Argentina
281) Sigmund Freud
282) Jay Anson
283) New Delhi
284) The Milky Way Galaxy
285) James Madison
286) Alfonso Cuarón
287) One billion years
288) Sir Edmund Hillary
289) Carbon
290) Skin
291) 9
292) Levi "Rivaille" Ackerman
293) Secretariat
294) Bikini Bottom
295) 1996
296) He
297) Adiós
298) A parliament.
299) Lima
300) Two
301) Unicorn
302) Ronald Regan
303) Kimchi
304) Spain
305) 1990
306) Traveler
307) Bela Lugosi
308) Georgia
309) Alcohol
310) Yuri Gagarin
311) Oven

312) Pug and Beagle

313) Hallo

314) Malcolm X

315) Three-fourths of the states (38 of 50)

316) Rip Van Winkle

317) Nike

318) Kate Winslet

319) 1968

320) The second Monday of October

321) Salt

322) Elephant (18 – 22 months)

323) Tobacco

324) Echolocation

325) Antarctica

326) France

327) Coffee

328) Margaret Mitchell

329) One

330) June

331) Nintendo Entertainment System

332) Chess

333) Mauna Loa (Hawaii)

334) Hola

335) Kim Jong Un

336) Sean Connery

337) Coulrophobia

338) Denver Broncos

339) Ryan Reynolds

340) Ireland

341) Stephen Hawking

342) Champagne

343) Australia

344) Eight

345) 538

346) Three

347) Qin Shi Huang (born Ying Zheng)

348) 88

349) Johnny Depp

350) Deoxyribonucleic acid

351) Nudity

352) Ambidextrous

353) Krypton

354) 10

355) Chris Cornell

356) National Collegiate Athletic Association

357) Beagle

358) Brunelleschi

359) Saint Augustine, Florida

360) Libertarian

361) Quentin Tarantino

362) Rhode Island

363) Hans Christian Andersen

364) Earthquakes

365) O3

366) Wonder Woman

367) Buddy Holly

368) Louisiana

369) Garage

370) Megalodon

371) Meg Ryan

372) Medusa

373) Nevada

374) Hawaii

375) Benjamin Franklin

376) Jazz

377) Frédéric Auguste Bartholdi

378) F. Scott Fitzgerald

379) 1926

380) Beak

381) Cosmo

382) Lady Gaga

383) Four

384) Michael Keaton

385) Venison

386) Boxing

387) 640

388) Link

389) Mercury

390) Tyrone Bogues, better known as Muggsy Bogues

391) 1789

392) Auguste Rodin

393) The whale shark

394) Serif Fonts

395) Portuguese

396) 5280

397) Light from the sun

398) Oliver Twist

399) Hollywoodland

400) The Dead Sea

401) Freddie Mercury

402) Scotland

403) The Rorschach test

404) Yeast

405) Blue

406) South Dakota

407) 2007

408) Craig MacTavish

409) The electromagnetic spectrum

410) The United States and Canada

411) 50

412) Raphael

413) Badminton

414) Rembrandt

415) Chameleon

416) Fifty

417) Lyndon B. Johnson

418) 2001

419) Liberty Island

420) Green

421) Seismometer

422) Budapest

423) Mr. Potato Head

424) Haggis

425) Sweden

426) Crises

427) Video Killed the Radio Star

428) The Arctic Ocean

429) John D. Rockefeller

430) John Lennon, Paul McCartney, George Harrison and Ringo Starr

431) Wind chill

432) Red Herring

433) Quesadilla

434) Texas

435) Four

436) Klick

437) Twenty

438) Bill Gates

439) Dalmatian

440) The Panama Canal

441) Zero

442) Random Access Memory

443) Alexander Graham Bell

444) 1978

445) Tequila

446) England

447) The Taj Mahal

448) Gamophobia

449) Captain Eugene Cernan

450) The Antarctic Polar Desert

451) The pituitary gland

452) Juan Ponce de Leon

453) Karaoke

454) Peregrine Falcon

455) Hypertext Markup Language

456) Portugal

457) Gone with the Wind

458) 1912

459) Salvador Dalí

460) Donkey

461) A cygnet

462) Plate Tectonics

463) University of North Carolina at Chapel Hill

464) Tokyo, Japan

465) London, England

466) Plain White T's
467) Spain
468) The Commodore 64
469) Marvin Gaye
470) Mandarin Chinese
471) Herman Melville
472) Malta
473) Origami
474) The Blair Witch Project
475) Charles Babbage
476) Queen Marie Antoinette
477) Solid, Liquid, Gas and Plasma
478) NaCl
479) Tom Kenny
480) Rome
481) Yellowstone National Park
482) Venus
483) Russian chemist Dmitri Mendeleev
484) Grover Cleveland
485) Hummingbird
486) Bobsled
487) The United States
488) Quebec City
489) California
490) Sun Tzu
491) The Canary Islands
492) Eucalyptus leaves
493) Hans Christian Andersen
494) Mercury
495) Washington D.C.
496) Supernova
497) Nike
498) William Hartnell
499) Phobos
500) Patrick Stewart
501) Paleontology
502) 1962
503) Captain Nemo
504) Columbus Day
505) An Amphibian.
506) The Red Baron
507) The Mayflower Compact
508) One, "The Red Vineyard at Arles".
509) 12 Monkeys
510) Uranus
511) Potassium
512) Kitten or Kit for short.
513) The Pacific Ocean
514) Earth
515) Jupiter
516) Two
517) Terabyte
518) The African elephant

519) Pyongyang
520) Chicago, Illonois
521) The Jazz Singer, released in 1927.
522) In the beginning
523) Norway, the other Nobel Prizes are awarded in Sweden.
524) 1993
525) The sperm whale has the largest brain weighing around 17 pounds.
526) Three with the Dallas Cowboys.
527) Ferdinand Magellan
528) State of Rhode Island and Providence Plantations
529) 88 MPH
530) Jupiter, it rotates once on average in just under 10 hours.
531) Charles Lindbergh in 1927.
532) French Riviera
533) John Hancock
534) Mark McGwire
535) California (Greenland Ranch, 134°F on July 10, 1913)
536) Thank you very much.
537) The Speaker of the House
538) Devils Tower in Wyoming
539) China with a land border of 13,743 miles (22,117 km).
540) "Under Pressure" by Queen and David Bowie,
541) St. Louis, Missouri in 1904.
542) The 1980 Oakland Raiders
543) Blackbeard
544) The Green Bay Packers
545) Annie
546) The Rolling Stones
547) England, Scotland and Wales
548) 1969
549) President John Adams
550) Nieuw Amsterdam (New Amsterdam)
551) Vatican City
552) Mark McGwire
553) Sarabi
554) A Flapper
555) Antarctica
556) New Zealand
557) James Earl Jones
558) 1995
559) 35
560) -40 degrees

561) Episode VI: Return of the Jedi
562) 2002
563) Oklahoma City
564) 1964
565) Pica
566) Philadelphia
567) Eighteen
568) Swifties
569) J. R. R. Tolkien
570) The Nobel Prize
571) Reply if you please.
572) 1927
573) Statler and Waldorf
574) Twelve
575) $25,000
576) Mediterranean Sea
577) Elephant
578) U2
579) Fore
580) Grain, hops, yeast, and water
581) France with 12 time zones.
582) Taiwan
583) The Great Pyramid of Giza
584) May 5th
585) Ponce de Leon
586) Skunk
587) Macy's
588) Donna Reed
589) George Orwell
590) Kentucky
591) Camel
592) Denmark, Dyrehavsbakken amusement park opened in 1583.
593) Venus (243 Earth days)
594) Russia
595) 32
596) Theodore Roosevelt
597) January
598) Diamond
599) White willow tree
600) $50
601) Vin Diesel
602) The Soviet Union
603) Kobe beef
604) Aphrodite
605) 1902
606) 1996
607) June
608) 1867
609) El Apóstol
610) Istanbul
611) Montana
612) Cinematographer

613) Patagonian toothfish
614) Femur
615) Sargasso Sea
616) 1892
617) Pete Best
618) Harry Belafonte
619) Cleveland Browns, Detroit Lions, Houston Texans and Jacksonville Jaguars
620) Four
621) 74 mph (119 km/hr)
622) The quick brown fox jumps over the lazy dog.
623) Independence Hall
624) New York City
625) Giraffe
626) President Franklin Delano Roosevelt
627) Corundum
628) Ferdinand Magellan
629) Venus & Uranus
630) Amelia Earhart
631) 2014
632) Mercury, Venus & Earth
633) Type O-
634) Hogwarts School of Witchcraft and Wizardry
635) Received
636) Boot Camp
637) Republican
638) 1024
639) Cheviot Hills
640) Alien
641) Vodka, Galliano and orange juice
642) World Series of Poker
643) Lennie
644) Gone with the Wind
645) Mormonism
646) Giant Panda
647) Claude Monet
648) The Large Hadron Collider
649) Lombardi's Pizza
650) Jacques Cousteau
651) Spruce Goose
652) Janet Jackson
653) Mars
654) The United States
655) The Burj Khalifa
656) Antikythera mechanism
657) I'll be back
658) Cricket
659) Madagascar
660) 13
661) French
662) Antarctica

663) John Lennon

664) The Orient Express

665) George Lucas

666) Eli Whitney

667) Michael Phelps

668) Australia

669) China

670) Karl Marx and Friedrich Engels

671) When a player scores three goals in a single game.

672) Will Smith

673) Vincent Van Gogh

674) Harper Lee

675) Fe

676) Ritchie Valens

677) Michelangelo

678) Angel Falls, Venezuela

679) A Murder

680) Sputnik

681) Jupiter

682) Tenerife

683) Albumen

684) Zero

685) 1967

686) Love Me Tender

687) Indian Ocean

688) Bill Gates

689) Happy, Sleepy, Sneezy, Dopey, Grumpy, Bashful and Doc

690) The Sun

691) You shall have no other gods before Me.

692) Andorra

693) 1787

694) Nitrogen

695) Cooperstown, New York

696) Knight Rider

697) Coca-Cola

698) 1945

699) Arnold Schwarzenegger

700) Pluto

701) Liberia, Myanmar and The United States

702) Norma Jeane Mortenson

703) 12

704) Nagasaki

705) Mary I

706) Hydrogen

707) 13

708) China

709) Dinero

710) Gravity

711) 24

712) 1492

713) 128

714) Avocados

715) 1896

716) United States Dollar

717) Amy Winehouse

718) Meteorite

719) ENIAC

720) Twenty Two

721) Vegemite

722) Leonardo DiCaprio

723) Christa McAuliffe

724) Ankara

725) Bitcoin

726) Hyper Text Transfer Protocol

727) John Adams

728) Moses Fleetwood Walker

729) H2O2

730) The Peach

731) Tina Turner

732) Pennsylvania

733) Canada

734) Blue Whale

735) The North Atlantic Ocean

736) Neil Armstrong

737) Mercury

738) Vatican City

739) Remember Me

740) Storm

741) Firearm

742) Knitting

743) 70 Meters

744) 36

745) Douglas Adams

746) Peter Sellers, April 1964 issue

747) Surfing

748) Eight

749) F=ma (Force equals mass times acceleration)

750) McDonald's

751) Rob Reiner

752) Andrew Johnson in 1868

753) Lock, stock, and barrel

754) Pigpen

755) Mt. Chimborazo in Ecuador (Due to equatorial bulge)

756) France (1924)

757) Eva Gabor

758) Aristotle

759) Silver

760) Pisa, Italy

761) 364

762) Ariel

763) Ostrich

764) 3.141

765) Venezuela and Ecuador
766) Bronies
767) Pumice
768) New York
769) Jack London
770) Shaking my hand
771) Three
772) King Cobra
773) Jim Carrey
774) Player Unknown's Battle-grounds
775) Ice hockey and lacrosse
776) Ukraine
777) Rudolf the Red-Nosed Reindeer. Adman Robert May first wrote of the now famous reindeer in a pamphlet distributed to children by store Santas in 1939.
778) Garfield
779) Mia Farrow
780) Grant Wood
781) Michigan
782) Frankie Valli
783) Abraham Lincoln
784) Mercury
785) Lego
786) Mars

787) Julia Louis-Dreyfus
788) Palindrome
789) Hemoglobin
790) Coach
791) Gerald Ford
792) Public house
793) Alaska
794) 206
795) Indonesia
796) Rob and Fab
797) Barenaked Ladies
798) High-Definition Multimedia Interface
799) Green, white and orange
800) Ohio (Dayton, Ohio was the home of Wilbur and Orville Wright)
801) Nathaniel Hawthorne
802) Arnold Palmer
803) Rami Malek
804) Venus and Serena Williams
805) Thailand
806) Hawaii
807) Lady Gaga
808) The Vegas Golden Knights
809) Lady and the Tramp
810) Bruce Lee
811) Medellin, Colombia

812) Giraffe
813) Margaret Thatcher
814) Wilt Chamberlain
815) An insane asylum (New York's Blackwell's Island Asylum)
816) The Emerald City
817) Melanin
818) It shredded itself
819) 45 rpm
820) Hamburg, Germany
821) Christopher Jones
822) Barry Bonds, with 73 home runs in 2001.
823) Epic Games
824) Hocus Pocus
825) Karl Benz
826) George III
827) New Orleans
828) Yiddish
829) The Krusty Krab
830) President Abraham Lincoln
831) Rainbow
832) 48 Hours
833) Calvin and Hobbes
834) Kiwi
835) Paris, France
836) Nine
837) Blue
838) Washington
839) Della Duck (called Dumbella in Donald's Nephews)
840) Argentina
841) The prison
842) Apple
843) Flying Fortress
844) The Attack on Pearl Harbor, December 7, 1941.
845) Bread
846) Axl Rose
847) Spain
848) Paraguay and Bolivia
849) New Hampshire
850) Duck or Goose
851) Golden Girls
852) Two
853) Trigger (originally named Golden Cloud)
854) Yellowstone National Park
855) The Federal Bureau of Investigation (FBI)
856) 32 Teams
857) Christopher Walken
858) 1993
859) Colin Kaepernick

860) Two (Jack & Meg White)
861) John Steinbeck
862) The finger lakes
863) Kwanzaa
864) Colombia
865) Captain Marvel (or Ms. Marvel)
866) Ben Affleck
867) Alex Trebek
868) Ian Fleming
869) Yellow
870) John F. Kennedy
871) Cincinnati Red Stockings
872) Non-commissioned officer
873) Sherlock Holmes
874) Shazam
875) Australia
876) The Great Barrier Reef
877) David Copperfield
878) Ralph Breaks the Internet
879) A brace
880) 14 Days
881) Black Sea
882) Christopher Lloyd
883) Australia
884) Central Perk
885) Armed Services Vocational Aptitude Battery
886) Shoes
887) Robert Edward Lee
888) Hail Mary
889) Ask Me Anything
890) Wild swine, pigs or boars.
891) The Nutcracker
892) Central Processing Unit
893) A Tale of Two Cities
894) Antoni Gaudí
895) Clue or Cluedo
896) Mixed Martial Arts
897) The Suez Canal
898) Seoul
899) A Connecticut Yankee in King Arthur's Court
900) Twitter
901) Lisa Valerie Kudrow
902) Route 66
903) Asia
904) Ford Motor Company
905) Cacti
906) Africa
907) Hawaii
908) Marie Antoinette
909) Never mind
910) Neptune
911) California
912) Marvel Comics

913) Ring of Fire
914) Humerus
915) Rome
916) Rocky III
917) Argentina
918) Apollo 11
919) Andy Warhol
920) Canada
921) Mark Twain
922) The bat
923) Rhythm and blues
924) Vulcanized rubber
925) Chili pepper (Capsicum annuum)
926) New York City
927) Men
928) Eight
929) Super Nintendo Entertainment System
930) Los Angeles Dodgers
931) Dean Martin
932) Mexico City
933) Butter
934) Lake Baikal
935) Tom Selleck
936) China
937) Meg Ryan
938) Blockbuster Video (Blockbuster LLC)
939) People's car
940) Ecuador
941) Ten
942) Jack Nicholson
943) Carne
944) Mount Aconcagua, Argentina
945) Bruce Wayne
946) Air France (AF) and British Airways (BA)
947) The Great Barrier Reef
948) California and Hawaii
949) The Bahamas (the Commonwealth of The Bahamas)
950) Joe Louis
951) Peru
952) Dennis Conner
953) Marsupial
954) Central Park
955) Rabbit Punch
956) The Purple Heart
957) $200
958) Daniel Dafoe
959) Bamboo
960) Yogi Bear
961) A trash can

962) Bucket list

963) Clouds

964) Ice cubes

965) Aretha Franklin

966) Murderer's Row

967) Spain and Portugal

968) Trees

969) Dandruff

970) Ecuador

971) Jurassic Park

972) Meteorites

973) Roller Derby

974) Liger

975) Walt Disney

976) Michael Collins

977) The Murray River

978) Nintendo

979) 50 Percent

980) Two

981) Sumo wrestling

982) The Paralympic Games

983) Randle McMurphy

984) Euclid

985) Captain Morgan

986) 50th

987) Molasses

988) Astro

989) Uranium (U92)

990) Oscar Meyer

991) China, Russia, and South Korea

992) Martin Van Buren

993) Guinness Book of World Records

994) Miley Cyrus

995) Smallpox

996) The Crimean War

997) The Battle of Puebla

998) Lionfish

999) Gregor Mendel

1000) Angola

1001) Mr. Clean

1002) Trigonometry

1003) De Beers

1004) Australia

1005) Blackjack

1006) Seize the day

1007) Diff'rent Stroke

1008) London, England

1009) Tennis

1010) Maple tree

1011) Italy

1012) Tyra Banks

1013) Methuselah: 969 years

1014)   Tim Robins in 2003 for Best Supporting Actor in Mystic River

1015)   Tom Hanks

1016)   1666

1017)   Ohio

1018)   Richie Havens

1019)   Louvre, Paris, France

1020)   Earl Monroe

1021)   Copper Mug

1022)   Fourteen

1023)   Led Zeppelin

1024)   Beaver

1025)   White Castle

1026)   Proxima Centauri

1027)   Elias

1028)   Panda

1029)   Japan

1030)   Harry S. Truman

1031)   Richard Nixon

1032)   Main Street, U.S.A.

1033)   Whiplash

1034)   Eddie Rickenbacker

1035)   Seven

1036)   Bobby Hull

1037)   Orion

1038)   Truman Capote

1039)   Uruguay

1040)   Vulture

1041)   Hypotenuse

1042)   Saint Patrick

1043)   Salmon

1044)   Shiba Inu

1045)   Facebook

1046)   Moby Dick

1047)   O+

1048)   Sumo

1049)   President Abraham Lincoln

1050)   Bavarian Motor Works (Bayerische Motoren Werke)

1051)   Hummingbird

www.ingramcontent.com/pod-product-compliance
Lightning Source LLC
Chambersburg PA
CBHW081723250726
48657CB00010B/3111